Hawaiian Memories

Blanche Howard Wenner

In the interest of creating a more extensive selection of rare historical book reprints, we have chosen to reproduce this title even though it may possibly have occasional imperfections such as missing and blurred pages, missing text, poor pictures, markings, dark backgrounds and other reproduction issues beyond our control. Because this work is culturally important, we have made it available as a part of our commitment to protecting, preserving and promoting the world's literature. Thank you for your understanding.

HAWAIIAN MEMORIES

Blanche Howard Wenner

Cochrane Publishing Company
Tribune Building
New York
1910

KD 47817

Copyright, 1910, by
COCHRANE PUBLISHING CO.

CONTENTS

	PAGE
Diamond Head	5
On the Old Moana Pier	6
To the Pali	8
The Dive	11
The Widow of Waikiki	12
The Trail to Tantalus	15
Hawaiian Garden	16
The Luau	17
The Makers of the Lei	18
Ode to Hawaiian Night	19
From a Surf Board	21
Hawaiian Morning	22
Molokai	23
Flying Fish	24
Reef Dreams	25
Hawaiian Singing	26
Amongst the Koa Trees	27
Kilauea	28
L'Envoi	29
Out of the Golden Gate	30

HAWAIIAN MEMORIES

DIAMOND HEAD

Great sentinel of tropic loveliness,
Titanic rock, clear cut in majesty,
Across whose rigid back the winds flow free,
Art thou the monument of that duress
Whence sprang the charm that lingering pilgrims bless,
The verdant islands guarded so by thee?
Or priest art thou for all that burdened sea,
Whose long blue waves at thy still feet confess,
Unchanging giant, well may scan thy mien
These people, ever luring pleasure sweet;
For thou, all gray amidst the gardens green
And golden quiver of the sunlight's beat,
Standest, as did that ancient Ark of Right,
Thro' storms unflinching in thy furrowed might.

HAWAIIAN MEMORIES

ON THE OLD MOANA PIER

To the heart of many a maiden
   Who has sojourned in Hawaii,
There's a spot forever laden
   With a smile and with a sigh.
So ho for the times so far and dear,
   When they wandered in the morning
      On the Old Moana Pier.

Then the violet sea was tumbled
   O'er the reefs and softly grumbled,
As the silver sands were crumbled
   In the sunlight hot and clear;
Then the distant palms were gleaming
   And the deeps with fish were teeming,
While her eyes in his were dreaming
      On the Old Moana Pier.

And the afternoon would find them
   Pacing o'er the foot-worn walk,
While the trade winds blew behind them
   Little jestings from their talk.
So ho for the times so far and dear,
   When they lingered in the sunlight
      On the Old Moana Pier.

HAWAIIAN MEMORIES

Then the distant ships arriving,
   And the breeze-blown palm-trees striving,
And the naked natives diving
   From the brown raft floating near,
Seemed but pictures strange and olden,
   Etched upon the sunshine golden,
All by them to be beholden
        From the Old Moana Pier.

Strange old pier, so long and silent,
   Stretching out to meet the sea,
You have harbored scenes quite violent
   (Tropic loves that quickly flee!)
So ho for the days so far and dear
   When they walked another dance out
        On the Old Moana Pier.

Then the lights were softly glowing,
   And the distant music flowing,
Through the shadows, deeper growing,
   Brought a wonder and a fear
Of "Aloha" softly ringing
   And the far surf's ceaseless singing,
While the tropic night came swinging
        O'er the Old Moana Pier.

HAWAIIAN MEMORIES

TO THE PALI

(On horseback)

I mount—we are off—my swift Lady and I,
  And the hard road beneath us in flashes doth fly.
I flee from the town and the soft dreaming heat;
  Now strike for the hills with your swift flying feet!

  Here steady, now, steady!
  The climb's yet to make,
  And I am not ready
  Your smooth neck to break!

On we swing, and the ring of her hoofs on the road—
The one sound all around—how it beats off my load!

  Cool breath from the banyan;
  We're nearing the canyon;
  Green rice fields below
  Like little squares show. Whoa!

Now wheel about, for one last look I'll turn.
  Behold the sea in silver sunlight burn;
Far to the left, straight from the reaches free,
  Rolls in the shining surf of Waikiki;
And in the vale, with royal palms above,
  Lies Honolulu, city of my love.

HAWAIIAN MEMORIES

Now on, my fine Lady, your spirit ne'er slacks!
　Feel the breeze in our faces, the sun on our
　　backs.
We have entered the canyon—ah, here's a good
　　place—
　With that hard road ahead—are you game
　　for a race?

　　What a wild rush of air!
　　How the rigid rocks flash!
　　Oh, the wind in my hair!
　　Slow, my Lady, you're rash.

I would see, as we flee, how the little green
　　trees
Wave and bend to the trend of the Pali's mad
　　breeze.

　　What a keenness it brings!
　　See, yonder are springs;
　　There's a shelter I know
　　From the wind's battle-blow. Whoa!

How clear the water is, how pure and cold!
　And high above the mountain, brown and
　　bold,
On whose far heights the speeding wind doth
　　rip,
　Seizing all things within his greedy grip;
And even the waterfalls he tears away,
　Throwing them upward in a wail of spray.

HAWAIIAN MEMORIES

Come, forward, my Lady, the Pali's ahead!
  We must stand on the brink ere the sunlight is dead.
There's a little cloud speeding adown the wind's train,
  And if I mistake not, 'twill drench us with rain.

    But away! We are glad
    Through the cloud's misty curtain
    To leap—'tisn't bad!
    But it's wet—that is certain.

Oh, I thrill to the will of the surf-scented shower—
Ah, at last it is past; how the sunlit cliffs tower!

    There's the gap and the ocean—
    Quick, charge this mad motion!
    'Tis the Pali's own blow.
    Here's the brink and below—Whoa!

How green and sweet the sugar cane's wide fields!
  How fresh the pineapples yon meadow yields!
While far away the brilliant, bounding sea,
  O'er whose blue surface sweep the trade winds free.
And this steep cliff, across whose edge they tell
  A conquered people struggled, fought, and fell!

HAWAIIAN MEMORIES

THE DIVE

He stands erect, slender and shining brown,
    The native boy;
Hands high, but eyes upon the sea bent down,
    Gleaming with joy.
He springs—a second's bronzy flash is seen—
Then swift he shoots into the sea's clear
    green.

HAWAIIAN MEMORIES

THE WIDOW OF WAIKIKI

(A ballad)

She was the widow of Waikiki,
  Little, blasé, and pert;
And her deepest plan was to snare a man
  For a moonlit evening's flirt.
But wasn't it sad for a gay Marine
  To awake with an aching head—
To have lost a girl with teeth like pearl,
  Thro' the lure of a parasol red?

'Tis a pleasant thing of an afternoon
  To sit on a long lanai,
And watch the surf boards skim the deep
  And the pretty girls go by.
Now he was a handsome officer,
  And a little bit swift at that,
And she was the widow of Waikiki,
  With cherries upon her hat.
She loitered by with a melting eye
  (Oh, the tropic day was warm);
And a little talk and a little walk
  Should never end in harm.
But out on the pier is a joysome place,
  In the sunset's tender light,
And an automobile and the Country Club
  Are nice on a tropic night.
So he sent for a brother officer,

HAWAIIAN MEMORIES

Who for fun was always game,
And they got a girl from the Orpheum
  To keep it from being tame.
So off they went, when the day was spent,
  And as over the road they sped,
The thought of the girl with teeth like pearl
  Had not yet entered his head.
Yet he was engaged to the preacher's daughter,
  Pretty, petite, and good,
Who walked in the straight and narrow path,
  As a preacher's daughter should.
And even that night she was waiting for him
  To sit on the small lanai,
Or to wander in father's garden,
  Under a starry sky.
But the Country Club (oh, there's the rub!)
  Is so charming a place, I ween,
That you never know where the minutes go—
  Alas! for the gay Marine!
For when he thought, in the midst of the feast,
  Of the maiden there alone,
In panic he rushed, with shaky legs,
  To call er up by 'phone.
And so mixed he was that his addled brain
  Thus wrenched the heart of the beauty:
"I am hopelessly detained, dear love,
  At the Country Club, *on duty!*"

HAWAIIAN MEMORIES

Now who would think that the glasses' clink
   The telephone wires won't cover?
And the words she said will buzz in his head—
   Until he finds another.

Oh the Country Club on its wonderful links
   Is a dangerous place to be,
And woman and wine and song, 'tis said,
   Are an officer's devils three;
But what is lost is lost, you know,
   And there's no use recalling,
And a host must do his best, you know,
   When the tropic moonlight's falling.
So a gay Marine and a swift machine
   And the ocean by them whizzes!
And the widow is "on" for a Marathon,
   In the wake of a few gin fizzes.

She was the widow of Waikiki,
   Little, blasé, and pert,
And her deepest plan was to snare a man
   For a moonlit evening's flirt.
But wasn't it sad for a gay Marine
   To awake with an aching head—
To have lost a girl with teeth like pearl,
   Thro' the lure of a parasol red?

HAWAIIAN MEMORIES

THE TRAIL TO TANTALUS

Come, comrade, we will strike the winding
    trail,
Where spicy odors on the sunlight sail;
The trail that leads 'neath the eucalyptus trees,
Whose silver shadows woo the brilliant breeze.
And there, with gray-gold lights to mantle us,
We'll sing our pæan to old Tantalus.
    So come, my friend.

'Tis quite a grade that we will have to make,
Ere that cold stream our climb-dried lips will
    slake.
But, oh, the zest in working towards the
    heights.
And looking down upon the valley's lights!
We'll see the rainbow o'er Manoa placed,
And slender mists of rain by sunlight chased.
    Then, comrade, come.

Nay, linger not; you know old Tantalus
Doth ever smile his welcome down on us
Since first together we achieved his crest
And sat upon his bare, cool heights to rest,
Commanding from his summit all of life,
Volcanic valleys, and the sea's far strife.
    Dear comrade, come.

HAWAIIAN MEMORIES

HAWAIIAN GARDEN

Breath of a full-blown blossom as it dies;
Scarlet hibiscus and white butterflies;
The ragged whisper of banana trees;
And far away the hiving hum of bees.
Cocoanuts falling where the sunlight gleams;
Soft folding of blue water flowers in dreams;
O'er Waikiki a gull upon the wing;
Silence—and in the garden Love is King.

HAWAIIAN MEMORIES

THE LUAU

(From a tourist's point of view)

Those natives in the garden—how they dig!
What! They are taking up the roasted pig?
(Or dog!) All swathed in shining leaves of ti!
Well, this looks like the very thing to me!
I say, dark maid, I haven't any fork
With which to test this charming piece of pork.
You don't use any! Really, pretty lass?
Well, then, that calabash of fruit please pass.
How charmingly "the Princess" doth preside.
(I wouldn't eat like this to save my hide!)
Some way upon the taste things seem to cloy.
What! Dip my fingers in this bowl of poi!
My appetite is gone—I wonder why!
If this lasts long, upon my word I'll die.
And now "the Princess" shares her perfume rare!
My handkerchief is ruined—Help, Lord—Air!

HAWAIIAN MEMORIES

THE MAKERS OF THE LEI

Through sun-bright hours in the narrow street,
Plucking the red carnations sweet,
Hard by the cool, gray curb they sit,
And thread the flower leaves bit by bit—
    The makers of the lei.

Dark old men who dream of the past;
Glib, fat women whose tongues run fast;
Working, gossiping, waving their flowers
At the passers-by through the fragrant hours—
    The makers of the lei.

Leis of yellow and red and blue
Their dusky fingers are flitting through;
Green-leaved leis that shine in the light;
And they smile o'er the ginger's scented white—
    The makers of the lei.

Scarlet leis they hang on their arms
For the Hula dancers' dusky charms;
Pink for the gay young lover's hat,
And they give an extra twist to that—
    The makers of the lei.

Leis to welcome the stranger guest,
And to bid God-speed the friends loved best;
Till it seems they cause in those leis to lie
The charmèd sweetness of old Hawaii—
    The makers of the lei.

HAWAIIAN MEMORIES

ODE TO HAWAIIAN NIGHT

O trancéd Night! Silver Hawaiian Night,
    Filled with the mysteries of all things
        sweet,
Here with the darkness touched, there with
        the white,
    Still veil of moonbeams wrapped about thy
        feet.
O voice of Passion answering the soul,
    And velvet hands that touch the spirit's
        wings,
And hold on high the purple starry scroll
    Whereon God's harmony forever sings!
Night, to the mystic throbbing of thy breast
    Gather my senses, calling out for rest.

Thou comest now, even as thou didst of yore,
    When the dark natives lived upon the isles,
Built their strange huts, and danced upon the
        shore,
    Tuning their music to thy saddest smiles.
And now, as then, thou sweep'st upon the
        light,
    Chasing it far across the round, dim sea,
And with the yearning sweetness of the night,
Gather'st the vèrdant islands close to thee.
So, for long hours they lie in thy embrace,
    While high above, the stars slip on through
        space.

HAWAIIAN MEMORIES

Of thee all wondrous, sweetest things are
        born,—
    The night song of the surf upon the reef,
And love's first whisper—stranger to the
        morn—
    And sleep that seals the heavy eyes of grief.
And that pure flower, the cereus, doth seem
    Like to a baby's soul, new-born, to lie
Within thy dusk, and like a maiden's dream,
    With the first distant breath of light to die.
Yea, they are highly sweet, these things of
        thine.
    Oh, through the spirit's kinship make them
        mine!

O Mother Night, moon-sweet Hawaiian Night,
    Beneath thy breath the tropic loves unfold,
Even as the cereus in its silver white
    And fairy fragrance,—and before the old
Worn light of days can mar it where it lies,
    So golden-hearted on the wall, it pales
And slips to death,—so quickly thy love dies,
    And all its strength in one deep night ex-
        hales!
And yet, more rare and precious seem those
        things
    Whose birth and death are compassed by thy
        wings.

HAWAIIAN MEMORIES

FROM A SURF BOARD

Closely I cling
To the wet, brown thing—
   And wait.
There's a green wave swinging
To soft foam singing—
   Now straight!

Point for the shore—HOLD TIGHT!
I travel fast on its emerald height,
And rise to my feet in the thing's wild flight.

Hands out—head back—clear the way!
I am drunk with the speed of the salt-tanged
   spray!
I am borne like a god on the water roar!
Slip—Plunge! *Ouf,* I must swim to shore.

HAWAIIAN MEMORIES

HAWAIIAN MORNING

Out of the silent wells of night
  Springs a little child of light.
Over the darkened arch of sea,
  Shod with sunlight wanders she.
And the gardens of Hawaii
  Lure her as she passes by.

There her freshest smile she brings;
  There her rarest song she sings;
Pouring there her sweetest balms
  To filter through the long-leaved palms.
Passes sadly on her way,
  Looking backwards all the day.

HAWAIIAN MEMORIES

MOLOKAI

("The Leper Island")

Far distant o'er the ocean's shining miles,
   In that sweet zone where all the shafts of sun
Leap fresh from the equator one by one,
   She lies alone, amongst her sister isles,
And every hour marks death upon her dials;
   While over them the moon-gay pleasures run,
Her web is of the darkest meshes spun,
   And on her hills a spirit army files.
O Molokai, upon whose verdant breast
   The still, white ghost of leprosy is nursed.
What sorrow hangs above thy sunlit crest!
   What voice of pain by thy sad surf rehearsed!
And yet, sweet stranger in the tropic sea,
   A tender, mother work is done by thee.

HAWAIIAN MEMORIES

FLYING FISH

Like instant, wingéd thoughts they leap
  To swift and iridescent flight.
A second gleaming way they keep,
  Then plunge into the sea's blue night.

HAWAIIAN MEMORIES

REEF DREAMS

I dreamed that all the still, sad tears
   My soul had wept away from thee
Had turned to silver phosphorus
   And floated on a tropic sea.

I dreamed that all the words we spoke,
   Through charmèd nights so long ago,
Had found their voices in the sea,
   And murmured on the corals reefs low.

I dreamed my soul was but a bloom
   Of cereus, so silver white,
And thine the strangely vibrant moon
   That found its golden heart one night.

HAWAIIAN MEMORIES

HAWAIIAN SINGING

O Life, that beats in every tone!
  No other cadences like those
Ever in my soul's palace rose—
  So gayly sweet and sadly lone.

One with the sun-green isles it seems:
  Beneath—the struggling, surging fires;
Above—the palm trees' windy lyres,
  Whose sweetness follows in our dreams.

HAWAIIAN MEMORIES

AMONGST THE KOA TREES

How sweet to dream amongst the koa trees
   There on the mountain's shoulder with the
       haze
Of Kilauea on the slow, blue breeze,
   Raising itself to meet the sun's keen rays.
       Yes, there to lie at length,
       Tingling with life and strength,
Stretched in the crooked lines of shade and
       light,
   And ponder on the koa forest bright.

How still it is! The sky of cobalt blue,
   The cool and golden sparkle of the air—
Is it through days like this the gnarled trees
       grew,
   And yet could find themselves no shape
      more fair?
       Or do those crooked limbs await
       Old Kilauea's kiss of fate,
Enwrapping them, even as those trees of old,
   Whose death we read in sunken lava mould?

And yet, a thousand years may come and go
   Ere that wild creature issues forth again;
And here upon this old tree fallen low,
   I lie and ponder things beyond man's ken.
       But oh, 'tis sweet to dream at ease
       Alone amongst the koa trees,
While far around the blue-gold charm doth lie,
   And clasps within its magic all Hawaii.

HAWAIIAN MEMORIES

KILAUEA

A silence desolate lies over all
  Those mist-hung leagues of hardened lava
    waves,
Whence a red beacon lures to those mad caves
  Where liquid light lashes its prison wall.
Held in the grip of nature's rocky thrall,
  Struggling for the far freedom that it craves,
Ever the mumbling mountain's side it braves,
  While winds blow back the smoke's titanic
    pall.
Oh, mighty force of God, oh, spawn of Life,
  Which deep within the earth's hot heart doth
    breed,
Searing our brains with thy convulsive strife,
  Here on these sea-far isles we pause and
    read,
While the pale pilot stars in their dim height
  Course quietly on o'er the red eye of Night.

HAWAIIAN MEMORIES

L'ENVOI

I will not say good-bye to thee,
   For he who once has been thy guest,
Though wandering far beyond the sea,
   Will seek again thy star-lit rest.
         Aloha!

I shall not even say good-night;
   Thou knowest sometimes nights are long.
Full measure I received of light;
   I give—these memories of song.
         Aloha!

HAWAIIAN MEMORIES

OUT OF THE GOLDEN GATE

Out of the Golden Gate, ahoy!
Out of the Golden Gate!
   Where the wild wind swings,
   And the spindrift sings,
And the strange, far countries wait.

I'll breathe no sigh for the Past, ahoy!
I'll breathe no sigh for the Past.
   For the furrow deep
   Shall charm my sleep,
And I am free at last.

Now let the pilot go, ahoy!
Now let the pilot go.
   For we must head
   To the sunset red,
Where the sea-tangled tempests blow.

So pull her to the West, ahoy!
Oh, pull her to the West!
   'Till the Cliff House fails
   And the coastwise sails
Are hid by the sea's white crest.

Then buck the bounding waves, ahoy!
Oh, buck the bounding waves!
   Let the phosphorus ball
   Through the black sea crawl,
Over the sailors' graves.

Let the old wind tear and rip, ahoy!
Let the old wind tear and rip,
   Till the bending spars
   And the mist-blind stars
Into the ocean dip.

HAWAIIAN MEMORIES

And hold her true all night, ahoy!
Oh, hold her true all night,
  Till we come through the dark
  Like the song of a lark,
  Chased by the dawn's far light.

Oh, my wandering's never through, ahoy!
My wandering's never through,
  While the tropics wait
  With the throb of Fate
Over the brimming blue.

Printed by Libri Plureos GmbH in Hamburg, Germany